Creating a Budget and Getting Out of Debt

A how to book on budgeting and debt relief.

Joshua J. Crouse

DEDICATION

This book of tools is dedicated to everyone. May each of you strive to become fore than you are, and all that you can be.

CONTENTS

INTRODUCTIONS

Many of us have found ourselves in situations, through no direct fault of our own, that have left us with an undeniable feeling of anxiety towards the future. Not knowing how you ended up in your financial situation and how you can dig yourself out of it are perfectly normal. It's normal and you are not alone. That is the first step you need to take to realize this situation is fixable. Within the following chapters I'll provide you with a chronological guide to the tools necessary for identifying, analyzation, and solution to your financial problems. Whether those problems stem from debt, poor credit usage, or just a lack of understanding when you're just starting out, you will learn something valuable about yourself and your goals. Sometimes even something as simple as writing a check for the first time can be confusing; But that is alright because I am here to help. Within this book I will cover what a budget is and why it's important, how to setup a budget, what to do once you've gotten yourself out of debt, and even how to write a check for the first time. My book is not just a "read it once and forget it" shelving decoration. It is a wealth of information to be taken down, used, and reused. In the final chapter I have provided you with a set of tools; pages you can copy, rip out, or print to use for the rest of your financial lifetime. These tools offer you the foundation you will require to put all your ducks together for a successful budget plan. As a bonus, Chapter 9 will focus on maintaining a credit rating that will set your future for success. To you, Reader, I say thank you for taking the time to realize your goals and go after everything you've always wanted. Good luck and let's get started.

1
WHAT IS A BUDGET AND WHY IS IT IMPORTANT?

A budget is an estimate of income and expenditure for a period. At least that's what Webster's has to say about it. For some the universal definition of what a budget is can be enough to get started. To those of us that require a more specific explanation, the textbook definition doesn't quite make the cut. To truly understand a budget and apply that science to your daily life we need to dig deeper. We need to know what constitutes income, expenses, and how it all works together to create a financial way of life.

The first step to understanding the dynamics of how a budget functions is within your income, or how much money you bring into your household. This can be calculated individually, or as a group if there are more than one income to your household. For the examples in this book I will just use an individual income and scale it out from there in Chapter 2. Even though there can be multiple incomes there are only two types of income.

The two types of income that individuals use to calculate income are "Gross" and "Net". Gross income is the amount you take in before any adjustments, deductions, or withholdings come out. For instance; If you make $10 per hour and work 40 hours per week, your Gross income is $400 per week, or $28,000 annually. How did I get those numbers? If you're not savvy to the realm of mathematics have no fear. The math here is simple, and I plan to keep it that way throughout this book. Below is a quick look at the 2 simple equations that give you Gross income.

Gross(weekly) = dollars per hour x hours worked
Gross Annual income = Gross(weekly) x 52 (the number of weeks in a year)

See, that wasn't so bad. Now we must tackle Net Income. Net can be a bit trickier if you're looking to calculate this all on your own by deducting your insurance, taxes, and any other expenses that come out of your paycheck before you receive it. However, most of that work is done for you by your employer. The amount you are paid at the end of each week, the actual amount that gets deposited into your bank account, is your Net income. This is the amount you want to work with when creating a successful budget for your household. A word on rounding numbers. If you want to round your numbers to the nearest dollar to make the math a bit easier to work with, go for it. Just remember to round your income down, and your expenses up. That way you don't get caught spending money you don't have.

The second piece of the budget puzzle is your expenditures, or expenses. An expense can be, quite literally, anything. From cable TV to gas in your car. Even dog food and movie nights if you attend them regularly. Any amount of money spent for anything on a regular basis will comprise a list of expenses. Expenses are where you really need to buckle down and get to the root of your financial situation. The key to calculating your expenses revolves around one simply concept; Reoccurring or repeating regular payments.

The repetition of a payment allows you to regulate when that money is, and is not, available to spend elsewhere. Which brings us to why a budget is important to know how to use, and to put into practice.

Since budgeting allows you to create a spending plan for your money, it ensures that you will always have enough money for the things you need and the things that are important to you; also known as Wants. Knowing the difference between a Need verses a Want is one of the most widely overlooked information when creating any budget. We all have that one friend that can't live without coffee. I know, I am that friend. However, a daily trip to the coffee shop, albeit qualifies as an expense, is not something that qualifies as a Need. Needs are the things that we, as human beings, require for basic survival; food, water, and shelter. Sometimes it can be difficult to separate the Wants from the Needs when you feel you've worked hard and deserve the best things in life.

This is precisely the purpose of a budget. To assist you in the quest for the best things in life. To procure your every desire so to speak. The other handy use for a budget is climbing out of holes. Not literal dirt, but the financial holes we sometimes find ourselves in. Following a budget or spending plan will also keep you out of debt or help you work your way out of debt if you are already there.

2
HOW TO CREATE A BUDGET THAT WORKS FOR ME

A budget only works if it works for you. Setting a budget that doesn't meet your needs or is far too aggressive can discourage even the most determined individual from achieving his or her goals. So be honest with yourself. I'll say it again. Be honest with yourself. The mistake made far too often is one that can be avoided right from the start. Being open and honest about how you spend your money will give you a clear look into problem areas that can be fixed when setting your budget goals. Start with the hard part. Expenses.

I like to divide this into two categories; Needs and Wants. Earlier you learned what each of those are and hopefully you'll be honest with yourself about which expense is a Need verses which is a Want. Categorizing your expenses like this will help later when we look at cutting down those expenses to better manage the bills or inflate your savings account.

Needs and Wants can be a hard-starting place for some, but that is precisely why we must start there. Making a list of where the income goes out is the first, and most important, step to detailing a successful budget plan. Without knowing where the income must be divided you will have a difficult time deciding what, if anything, you have let over for savings and fun.

Determining your income is a close second when it comes to order of importance. Without it, our needs and wants just don't happen at all. Your income is the lifeblood of your ability to exist amongst society. It determines how you eat, what you wear, drive, and even if you take the family on a holiday for the summer. Take great care in calculating your income. As we discussed earlier, don't bother to include money that you will never be able to use for something else. It is tempting to write down a $50,000/yr. income, but if you can only send $30,000 you are only cutting your budgets legs out from under it. Remember, you're doing this to improve your life and take it in a direction that focuses on what is truly important.

Decide what is and is not important to you before you try to budget out different expenses. Take ten or fifteen minutes to reflect on what you want out of life. What direction you would like it to go and write down some financial goals. Seriously, go do it right now. This book isn't going anywhere on its own. I'll wait…

Good. Now that you've taken the time to ponder what it is you'd like to get out of this exercise we can continue.

Write down some of those goals below this paragraph. This is going to help solidify those goals in your mind. If you've just got one, that's okay. Write that one goal really, really, big. After you've done it, we'll start on the actual work. It begins with determining your income.

3
DETERMINING YOUR INCOME

Income is any amount of money that get deposited into your bank account on a regular basis. Determining your income will be the easiest part of setting up your budget. Whether it be job income, social security, retirement, or payouts from financial assets this is all spendable within your budget. Even child support and food share programs can be, and should be, considered income when you're designing the perfect budget.

The first task you'll need to accomplish is to list them all out and get a total for each month. Remember, the Net income is what you want to list here, not the Gross. There's no point in writing down money that you can't allocate to different places. If you are going to round the numbers, round down to the nearest dollar. This way you don't end up adding in change you don't have. If might not seem like much but even pennies can cripple a good budget over time. Below here, or on a separate piece of paper, list those income sources that apply to your family.

After you've listed them, add them together. This will provide you with all the income data you'll need. When looking at your paychecks for your income be sure to use the net amount. The amount that was deposited into your bank account.

The next step would be to make sure your income is converted into a number we are able to work with easily. Most people pay bills monthly, so that is the standard we will be using throughout the budgeting process. Your annual income can be broken down by dividing it by twelve. For example, if you're annual income is 50,000:

50,000 divided by 12 = Monthly income.

Again, remember to use numbers that are net (after everything has been subtracted before if goes into your bank account).

4
CALCULATE EXPENSES

Take out a piece of paper and divide it into two sections. Start writing all your Needs in one section and the Wants in the other. The Needs category will consist of anything that can be defined as Food, Water, or Shelter. The Food items are self-explanatory. Most people have some idea of how much they spend each week or each month on groceries. If you collect receipts, then you're already one step ahead of the game. If not, it's a good habit to get into.

Collecting receipts will better serve you in the future when you need to adjust or recalculate your budget plan. Collect the receipts every time you go to the grocery store, order out, grab a snack, or eat at a restaurant. Put all those receipts into an envelope. If you do this for an entire month, you'll be able to get a better idea as to exactly how much you spend monthly on food items. Be sure to write on each receipt how many other people you bought food or drinks for. This way you'll know exactly why you bought multiple sodas or an entire pizza instead of just one slice.

Cutting down your expenses can be as simple as telling the friend or co-worker you always pay for that it's time, they buy their own lunch. Drinks out with friends can be another problem place for someone who has a generous nature. Which brings us to the next Need. Water.

Water is likely a utility that you pay regularly, or it may be included within your rent. If it is, then no need to try and figure out exactly how much water you use and the calculated cost of usage. If not, most water utilities are calculated monthly or quarterly. If yours happens to be one that is billed quarterly just take your latest bill and divide that by three. This will give you a monthly estimate for your budget.

The next important item on the list is shelter. This expense is, by far, the most important. It is your home. The place in which you feel safe, keep your most personal possessions, and raise your family. Make sure this is always a priority. Under the Needs category write down all the associated expenses with your home. This can include rent, mortgage, electric and gas utilities, sewer (if separate from water), and garbage pickup. These are all expenses that cannot be overlooked. They must get paid. Period.

Another need is transportation. In today's world you most likely drive to work every day, or at the very least ride a bus. When calculating your vehicle costs don't forget your loan payment, or insurance if you live in one of those states that it has become a requirement. If you don't, it's still a good thing to have and, in my opinion, falls into the Need category.

Another set of expenses people neglect are the maintenance costs that go along with vehicle and home ownership. Your oil needs to be changed, tires, brake pads, and the like. To break these into monthly expenses you just need to know the recommended time between services. For example, most oil changes should be done, typically, every 3 months. Meaning that if your oil change is $30 you would divide that by 3 to find out how much to set aside each month.

Credit card payments are another big one. If you've got them, be sure to write in the minimum payments for each card. Another good example of a Need would be your healthcare. If this is deducted out of your paycheck, don't worry about putting it down, but if you pay for it privately be sure to list it under the Needs category. This is not something you should have to give up.

Moving beyond your Needs you can now begin to list your Wants. This can be anything recurring. Internet, cable or satellite TV, streaming sites, date nights, absolutely anything you spend on a regular basis. This is where you put your morning coffee, donut, or sandwich one the go. The Wants category is strictly for your habitual spending items. The one's you tell your co-workers you can't live without.

5
AM I IN DEBT?

First, determine if you are, in fact, in debt. This seems straight forward, but there is a difference between "being in debt", and simply living beyond your means. What do we mean when we say, "living beyond your means"?

Living beyond your means is determined by how much income you have and how much you spend. It's a simple ratio. If you have direct deposit to your back, often, it is simple to figure this out. Look at your last bank statement. It should list both the amount deposited for the month, and the amount debited (or withdrawn) for the month. Subtract the Debit from the Deposits. If you get a negative number, you're living beyond your means.

Simply put, you spend more than you have. That part of your life needs to be put to a stop if you're ever going to relieve yourself of debt. If you fall into the category of people living beyond their means, you'll likely have accumulated significant debt just trying to stay ahead of your bills. Let's break it all down and see what we can do about that.

First, you'll need to do some information gathering. In the table below list all your bills; mortgage/rent, utilities, gas, food, credit card minimum payments, school fees, streaming accounts, and the like. List anything reoccurring each month.

Name of Account/type	Minimum Payment

After listing each individual payment, you make each month, add those numbers to get a Total Monthly Bill Statement and enter that amount here _____. We will use this number to both minimize monthly expenses and calculate how much we can allocate towards paying off outstanding loans and bad debt. Bad debt, to us, is anything that incurs interest or has a past due amount.

Make a list of any bad debt that can be paid off. This will help us determine how much you owe and begin to create a plan to get this debt paid off. Remember, your goal here is to get out of debt so you'll have to make some sacrifices. Be prepared to let a few luxuries go if you want to tackle this debt in a timely manner.

Name/Account Type	Total Amount Owed as of Date:_____

6
HOW TO GET OUT OF DEBT

Now that you've determined that you fit into the "in debt" category you can begin to do something about it. We need to setup a Debt Payment Plan. A Debt Payment Plan is a calculated payment plan that you setup based on your personal income to debt ratio that allows you to pay off debt within a specific frame of time.

Set up a Debt Payment Plan. ...

Use the following planner to write down your Payment plan. Remember, you must stick to it so make sure your payment plans are responsible and reasonable. Be realistic. Create one for Each of your debt accounts. I've provided you with a few that will help you get started. There are a few things you can do to help free up some extra cash for your repayment plans. Here is a brief list to get you started.

1. Lower Your Debt to Income Ratio. We covered this in the previous chapter. Sacrifice what you do not need and cancel what you do not want. ...

2. Pay Off Old Debt. A great goal is to pay off old debts that you have let go. If you owe a debt that

13

you can pay off within 1 or 2 checks, do it. Start with the oldest and work your way to the most recent. ...

3. Stop Using Credit Cards inefficiently. There is a right way to use credit. Paying your American Express with your Visa isn't it. Keep your balances below 30%. This is known on your credit report as "Usage". Always pay more than the minimum (even just one dollar), and if at all possible, pay off your cards each month before your reporting date. ...

4. Find Lower Interest Rates Through Balance Transfers. This is a tricky one, but it works. If you find a credit card with a lower interest rate and can pay off a card with a higher interest rate, do it. This will help keep your interest payments low. Just remember not to max out even a low interest card for this. That can do just as much damage to your credit rating. Always, always, always ask for an increase in your credit limit every 6 months on every card. The higher your limit, the easier it is to maintain a lower balance. ...

Refinance whenever possible. Car loans and Mortgages can really dip into your pockets when the interest rates skyrocket. So, fight back and refinance whenever possible for a lower rate. ...

Debtor (Name of Company)			
Total Amount Owed			
Minimum Payment			
Interest Rate			
Date	Starting Balance	Payment	Remaining Balance

7
SETTING GOALS

Now that you've got your basics down you can start setting some goals for yourself. Your savings account should be just that. It's for saving towards a goal, not for spending. Savings is for the unexpected expense, college for the kids, or an annual vacation to get away from it all.

Your savings can, and should, be divided into two categories as well; Long term and short-term accounts. Long term accounts should be kept out of site and out of mind. Long term savings accounts are best when not linked to your regular accounts online. I prefer to use a separate bank entirely. This helps us to keep that extra cash we have out there "out of mind". Savings accounts are meant to be inflated rather than used. These are typically an account for college funds, new homeownership down payments, and anything you might need a year, or more, to save over a long period of time.

Short term savings accounts are for the fun stuff. This is where you put your vacation, new car, motorcycle, boat, and RV money. Anything you can save for within a year should be put into these accounts. Over and above the big-ticket items your saving for a good rule of thumb is always to keep six months' worth of bills(needs) in your savings account. This may seem like a daunting task but getting there just takes a bit of time. Which is why you're setting your budget in the first place. To get your finances in order.

When setting your savings goals, you need to be realistic. It is unlikely that you will be able to save $10,000 in three months even if you bring home $40,000 per year. It's not impossible either. Set your savings goals realistically. Start with the six-month rule. Give yourself one year to save up six months' worth of bills to prepare for that just in case situation. If, after you've ran your numbers you can do it in less time, then you can adjust your timeline. Time and time again I've witnessed intelligent people just like you set themselves up for failure because they tried too hard too quickly. Saving money takes time. Allow for that time to solve your debt and savings goals for you. Let time do all the hard work while you enjoy the benefits.

Spending limits help greatly with savings goals. The two go together when you want to ensure the long-term viability of your budget. Spending limits is, in my experience, the most difficult aspect of a budget to stick to. Partly, you ended up here because you did not adhere to your spending limits. We've all done it. You walk into the grocery store to get a pound of hamburger or a loaf of bread, and you walk out with a soda, snack for the kids and yourself, maybe a magazine, lighter, headphones, or whatever other random something or another that caught your eye on the way out. It's okay. If snacks are your thing, just build them into your budget. Remember, the goal isn't to punish yourself, but to create a plan that helps you spend your money on the things you want without feeling anxious about rent, or a car payment at the end of the month. If you are like me and you have a rough time with sending limits, then this section should be your personal financial bible. Read it twice, three times, in the morning, and before bed. The best way to discover problem areas and start setting spending limits is to figure out what you spend and where you spend it.

Record spending and track progress. ...

It may seem like a hassle to record everything, but this is where the work starts and the problem solving begins. A small notebook or ledger to record your spending. Each time you make a purchase, write down the date, items, and prices. Keeping each receipt and doing this at the end of each day inputting the data into a spreadsheet on Excel is ideal, but you can always do this with pen and paper if you're not familiar with Excel.

On the next page I've put together a table you can copy to use. This will help you get started developing the habit. Recording your transactions should become routine if you truly want to stick to your goals and always be on top of your financial situation. Each row is broken into five columns; Location(the store you bought the item in), Item Description(record what the purchase was for; food, toys, utilities, snacks, gas, or whatever it was that you purchased), Amount $(record the cost of the item or items after tax; there will never be a time when you aren't spending that tax amount so it should be part of the budget), the Date, and if this item falls under the "Need" or "Want" categories. Remember, being honest with yourself here is the key to a successful budget.

Spending Record Sheet				
Location	Item Description	Amount $	Date	Need or Want

Below categorize your Needs vs. Wants to start getting a picture of what can or cannot be sacrificed.

Need	Want

Total amount in the Need category _____

Total amount in the Want category _____

    If your Wants category is more than your Needs category, than you have done this correctly. Thank yourself.

    Start thinking very hard about the goals for yourself and your budget. Everything in the Wants category can be a sacrifice to your debt, or savings accounts. Really consider if something is worth it or not, can you consolidate any of those items into one, do you even use some of the items on that list? Take a good look at your list and start to pin down where your budget is hemorrhaging unnecessary money.

    I once helped a family realize they had been making a twenty-dollar payment each month for a subscription they forgot they had. This went on for years. They had paid over $3,000 towards a bill they didn't even realize they had just because it was an automatic withdrawal they forgot to turn off. The lesson here is nothing should be on autopilot except your Needs. Don't set yourself up for this sort of bad news later in life.

    When you go down the list of Needs, put everything on automatic payments that you can. I prefer to setup a bank account solely for this purpose. Each pay period direct deposit $5 more than your Needs total. This ensures there is always enough. You will likely never have to worry about your electricity getting shut off if you setup this simple fail-safe. Below, list all the items you want to cancel. After you do this, stop. Go and cancel those things before you continue with this book and put a nice big check mark next to each one when it is done.

    Total Amount of Payments you will no longer be making $_____

    Did that feel good? It should. The number you just wrote down is now how much you've saved with a simple cancellation. This is the first number we can begin to divert into savings, or debt relief. Remember the income math we did earlier? This is where it all comes together.

    Use the Net income you calculated from earlier to determine where you stand with your new income to expense ratio.

    Income – Expenses = What you must work with.

Put your new budget number here $_____.
This is free income you can divert to a savings account of your
choosing. Congratulations, you've made the first step to being in
control of your financial situation.

8
DESIGN YOUR BUDGET

Now that you've gathered all your data and you've learned a thing out two about finances, and yourself. You can begin to put together your budget.

Analyze your spending and set a budget using the table on the next page.

Weekly Budget Planner		
Category	**Weekly Budget**	**Total**

In each box place the category that the amount you would like to allocate, or set aside, for that category. Categories are things like rent, food, fun, or savings. The best option is to take the Needs list from earlier and allocate those funds first. Then, use the remainder to fill in where you'd like to have a few extras.

I prefer to use separate bank accounts for my wants and my needs. My needs get direct deposited into an account that is strictly for those things that must be paid. Each week, an amount five dollars more than I need is deposited into those accounts. I never have to worry if there is enough money for my bills, because it's allocated before I ever see it.

For fuel in my car, I use prepay cards that I put only what I want to spend on each week. If I plan a longer trip, I restrict my usage in the weeks prior so that I don't go outside my fuel budget. The same is true for groceries, and other sometimes fluctuating expenses. Whenever possible I link automatic payments to a prepaid card for things like, internet, television, streaming, or music apps. This way, if I always know what is getting paid and what I have left.

Each year I zero out my needs account. Remember, there is an extra five dollars deposited each week. This money I either send over to my savings or use it to splurge on something random I've had my eye on. No matter how you decide to setup your finances, just remember to stick to the budget. It can be rough at times, but it will be worth it in the end.

Congratulations, now that you've read my book, you're magically debt free! Nope, unfortunately it doesn't work that way. Now the real work begins. Use this book as a reference to get that debt and budget under control. Remember, this book is meant to be a tool referred to regularly. You've got this and you're the only one that can change your situation. If you would like personal counseling on your specific situation, I've included some links, references, and contact information to professional services that are always willing to help.

To some degree we all have been in a situation when our finances have become more of a prison than the freedom we were promised as a child. Never fret over what you cannot control. All my life I was told repeatedly, but I never truly understood what it meant until I was able to learn how to control the individual apparatus that makes my life what it is. Your individual finances are completely, and undeniably, in your control. I hope that you've learned a thing or two by this point and can practice at home what I've managed to preach here in this book. I'll leave you with a few parting tips to help you along the journey. The following will be covered in more detail with book 2 of this 3-book series on Individual Finance.

1. Manage credit card balances based on cash on hand. ...

2. Monitor spending with a self-imposed credit limit. ...

3. Limit housing expenses. ...

4. Pay yourself first. ...

5. Make it your mission to avoid unnecessary fees. ...

6. Don't give your budget a raise.

Debt can be intimidating, but it doesn't have to be demoralizing. If you would like help with your finances, there is help there. Type in this link and get the help you need from a Professional.

Www.dreamsfinancial.wixsite.com/website

9

MANAGING A CREDIT SCORE

Managing your credit score can be an easy task if you allow it to be. Follow these simple rules.

1. Do not use more than 30% of your available limit per credit line. For loans, try to pay them down below 30% as fast as possible. Then, refinance and repeat.
2. Always pay your bill on time, or early. If you can pay your balance off before your reporting date, do it.
3. Don't waste your time allowing someone to make inquiries into your credit if you are unsure if you even want the item. Ask what the range of scores they typically see approved before you allow someone to run an inquiry.

Set dates for getting your credit reports. Annually, you should check each of your credit reports. You should spread out your requests, making requests once per quarter, so you can catch errors that might come up at different parts of the year and spot potential identity theft. By maintaining these dates over time, you can mark them as a recurring event in your Palm Pilot or on your calendar.

Get your credit score once a year. A credit score is a three-digit number that reflects the credit history detailed by a person's credit report. Every year, you should try to look at your credit score from one or all the three credit bureaus. There are a vast number of services out there, and apps, that allow checking up on your score to become even daily.

Lock up cards; don't cancel them. Do whatever it takes to limit your use of credit cards, but don't cancel credit card accounts once they're paid off. Why? Because your credit score relies on the number of credit lines you have open and in good standing and the length of time, they're open. Keep in mind the ones that have regular fees and make sure those are paid on time. Lenders want to see a long record of credit management, and longtime accounts you haven't touched in years may help your score by showing you have some restraint. Remember to use them once a year and pay the full amount off immediately to keep credit cards active.

Pay on time. Nothing damages your credit standing faster than late payments, particularly on big loans like mortgages and car payments. It's extremely important to get current and pay in advance of the due date. Electronic bill paying eliminates mailing delays and gives you the ability to better manage payment dates. If paying by mail, I suggest mailing the payment five to seven days before the due date. Regardless of how you pay bills, it's a good practice to enter all bill due dates in your calendar.

Monitor credit problems. If you've filed for bankruptcy or had a debt put in collection, it takes years to remove those events from your credit record. Determine the month that data should leave your report and make sure you follow up to make sure that removal happens.

Choreograph your payments. If you have multiple balances you need to eliminate, schedule a payment order starting with the highest-rate balances first. You should also consider the oldest. If you have several small debts on your report that are easily paid off, take care of those first.

Keep your balances low. If you carry balances more than 30 percent of your credit limit on any account, it might lower your credit

score. To remedy this, use several cards to spread out the balance--
and pay them off--or ask the creditor to raise the limit on the card.

Limit your credit inquiries. Credit inquiries from potential lenders,
solicited or unsolicited, can lower your score. This includes mortgage
companies every time you get pre-approved and department stores
that offer you a 10 percent discount if you open a charge card. This
also applies to unsolicited credit card offers you receive in the mail.
It's a good idea to remove yourself from direct mail lists.

Research big loans in advance. Always ask a potential lender
which credit bureau they use to make their decisions. Auto, mortgage
and other lenders may prefer one credit bureau over another. So, if
you plan of your large purchase in advance, you should aim to correct
errors in your credit report and get your credit score as high as
possible. This will also avoid an unnecessary inquiry from a lender
that you knew would not have approved your situation.

Track your credit card spending. If you've never tried to track
your credit card spending, do so starting this credit cycle. It can be as
simple as a paper list or as sophisticated as a spreadsheet or money
management software. Whatever tool you choose, tracking your
spending will give you a forecast of your upcoming monthly bill. You
can also track your recent charge card activity directly at the issuer's
website. The goal is to know what your payment will be so that you
can plan accordingly. Tracking will also allow you to notice
fraudulent charges well in advance before they become a true
nightmare.

These may seem like simple tricks or things you may have already
heard before, but they can be the difference between an 800 and a
450-credit score.

10
WORKSHEETS AND TOOLS

The following are various worksheets and tools used throughout this book. Use them for your purposes of maintaining your financial freedom and growing your wealth. Thank you for taking the time to read my book and good luck to you all.

Gross(weekly) = dollars per hour x hours worked
Gross Annual income = Gross(weekly) x 52 (the number of weeks in a year)

Debtor (Name of Company)			
Total Amount Owed			
Minimum Payment			
Interest Rate			
Date	Starting Balance	Payment	Remaining Balance

Weekly Budget Planner		
Category	**Weekly Budget**	**Total**

Weekly Budget Planner		
Category	**Weekly Budget**	**Total**

ABOUT THE AUTHOR

Joshua J. Crouse has been Entrepreneur, Author, Student, and Teacher. Although most of his life was spent working labor positions, he took it upon himself to learn, and grow to become more than he ever thought he could be. His experience, both in the fields of finance and family, offer a great wealth of knowledge and experience. Coming from modest means he strives to help everyone that he reaches to live better, happier lives through financial coaching, advice, and his friendship.